These questions are answered by:

All your answers are not wrong
All your answers are not always right
All come from your bright or dark thoughts
All come truly, deeply from your heart and soul
And all come to define who you are at this very moment

DAY 1

How do you stay calm and collected?

DAY 2

How would you make your first date better?

DAY 3

What's the scariest thing you have ever seen yourself do?

DAY 4

What's your greatest joy?

DAY 5

What are some things that are okay to occasionally do but not okay to do every day?

DAY 6

What makes you think that a person as smart as you are incapable of understanding some things?

DAY 7

What is your most important desire right now?

DAY 8

How do you deal with a man whose sole mission in life is to make you fall off the ledge?

DAY 9

How would you describe the feeling of being up there on stage?

DAY 10

If you could build your dream house right away? Which house would it be?

DAY 11

If you had to choose one breed of dog to add to your family, which would you choose?

DAY 12

How do you deal with a breakup?

DAY 13

What is your story and where is it going?

DAY 14

If you could listen to any song that no one has ever heard before, what would it be?

DAY 15

What was it like to hear that in the past year?

DAY 16

List of things that people have asked me

DAY 17

What is the best way that you've ever been treated by somebody?

DAY 18

If you could give a small favor to anyone in the world, what would it be?

DAY 19

What's your most treasured memory from high school?

DAY 20

If you could get rid of all the things in your life that aren't fun, what are those things?

DAY 21

What is the one thing that you've seen you do right that other people can't do?

DAY 22

Which is your worst relationship?

DAY 23

What is one thing you love about your life?

DAY 24

Explain the problems, both personal and societal, that result from obesity.

DAY 25

What story have you lived the most?

DAY 26

List of things that have occurred to you

DAY 27

Describe a time when you received a valuable gift.

DAY 28

How do you deal with these kinds of stories that happen so quickly?

DAY 29

How would you describe the feeling of being in a position to save people who couldn't save themselves?

DAY 30

List of things that men shouldn't be allowed to be

DAY 31

What does your biggest contribution mean to someone else?

DAY 32

Are you eating enough protein? Why?

DAY 33

How would you describe the feeling of being misjudged?

DAY 34

What is the most terrifying thing you have ever seen?

DAY 35

Talk about your worst birthday celebration of all time.

DAY 36

How do you keep calm in stressful situations?

DAY 37

Tell about a time when you were hurt by something you didn't know.

DAY 38

Is it something I need to do again? Why?

DAY 39

What are some disappointments you had in your life?

DAY 40

Which parent are you closer to and why?

DAY 41

How much do you rely on luck?

DAY 42

What do you want your parents to know about you?

DAY 43

What's the biggest personal change you've ever made?

DAY 44

Would you rather be riding a heavy dragon or a light unicorn? Why?

DAY 45

Why do you think it'll feel like?

DAY 46

What is the most significant new thing you've learned?

DAY 47

Name a public figure who has inspired you? Why?

DAY 48

If you found a treasure worth millions in your backyard, would you keep it a secret or would you tell the world? Why?

DAY 49

Would you rather be yourself or more?

DAY 50

What should you expect from this?

DAY 51

How do you teach your children how to make themselves feel better (when they're feeling bad)?

DAY 52

Would you ever take back someone who cheated?

DAY 53

List of things that I probably need to understand

DAY 54

What is the craziest thing one of your teachers has done?

DAY 55

If your life depended on it, what would you change?

DAY 56

What is your favorite type of ice cream?

DAY 57

If you could only write down your nightmares, what would it be?

DAY 58

Do you prefer the dark and the strange? Why?

DAY 59

If you had to choose one thing to do in your life right now that would bring you happiness, what would you pick?

DAY 60

What would you prefer to see next?

DAY 61

What would you do if someone told you a joke that you don't think is funny?

DAY 62

What is the most important aspect of your life and why?

DAY 63

Have you made any significant breakthroughs in the last few years that helped you or changed who you are?

DAY 64

Who are your favorite heroes?

DAY 65

If you had to choose one thing from the entire year for a favorite memory, what would it be?

DAY 66

What is the point of your journey today?

DAY 67

What would you give up to have what you do?

____

____

____

____

____

DAY 68

What phrase is so iconic that everybody instantly knows who said it?

____

____

____

DAY 69

How would you describe the feeling of being attracted?

DAY 70

*If you had to choose one thing to be the most important lesson
I've learned along the way, what would it be?*

DAY 71

*If you had to choose one thing you would want to change if
you had to start over, what would it be?*

DAY 72

What is the current state of things in your life?

DAY 73

What are your five most embarrassing times in the spotlight?

DAY 74

How do you know when you're alone?

DAY 75

How would you describe the feeling you get in a room full of people who can all just come up with the most astonishing examples of fantasy?

DAY 76

What are you really waiting for?

DAY 77

What's the most important thing that's happened to you today?

DAY 78

What makes you feel sad or can easily drive you to desperation?

How do you deal with anxiety?

How would you describe the feeling of being up in the mountains?

What languages do you speak?

DAY 82

Tell us a time you were really sad.

DAY 83

What is one thing you have in common with your grandson?

DAY 84

What do you think is the reason you have the best relationship with your parents?

DAY 85

List of things that you are interested in

DAY 86

How can this world be better for kids who aren't even born yet?

DAY 87

What makes people not do or act the way they should do?

DAY 88

When did you have your first panic attack?

DAY 89

What is the name of your favorite song?

DAY 90

*How do you deal with the fact that the way your body
functions is so different from everyone else?*

DAY 91

What's the most embarrassing thing that people have done to you?

____

____

____

____

____

DAY 92

What was the hardest thing about your relationship?

____

____

____

____

DAY 93

What will you be most proud of in your life?

What is your greatest strength?

Describe a time when you accomplished something you didn't think you could do.

How would you define your art?

DAY 97

If you had to do three things today, what would you do?

DAY 98

List of what's in my wallet

DAY 99

If you could be born and brought up in the world of the occult, what would you do?

DAY 100

What are your most inspiring daily mantras?

DAY 101

If you want something so bad that you will destroy yourself to protect it, what would you be willing to sacrifice for it?

DAY 102

What is something really popular now, but in 5 years everyone will look back on and be embarrassed by?

DAY 103

Do you stop worrying about people? Why?

DAY 104

What does someone do when they're feeling anxious? Why?

DAY 105

How would you like to spend your time?

DAY 106

What does your child like to do when he/she's bored?

DAY 107

Tell us something that's missing in your hometown.

DAY 108

Have you ever had an intense emotional reaction to music?

DAY 109

List of things that would end a game

DAY 110

How would you describe the feeling of being part of something?

DAY 111

Are you always getting into your own head?

DAY 112

What makes you most attracted to someone?

DAY 113

If you could pick your two greatest heroes in movies, who would they be?

DAY 114

When have you felt lonely?

DAY 115

Do you have any bad feelings about yourself? What are those?

DAY 116

If you could be just one person who no one could ever forget, who would it be and why?

DAY 117

Tell the story of what you were doing when you heard about an important event and how that news affected you.

DAY 118

Why is it not the best way to live?

DAY 119

Which is more important to you, to get out there and keep walking, or to spend so much time on the phone with people who hate you that you're disconnected from your life?

DAY 120

Will you be like others or will you be different? Why?

DAY 121

What causes you to do the things you do?

DAY 122

What are some of your favorite places to work?

DAY 123

What makes you feel super loved?

DAY 124

How do you deal with your emotional outbursts?

DAY 125

Do you have a favorite memory of your relationship? Why?

DAY 126

How do you encourage your children to take responsibility for their own choices?

DAY 127

What is the one thing you do not wish to ever see again?

DAY 128

What were the most difficult things you were told about your life growing up?

DAY 129

What is one thing you look forward to at Christmas time?

DAY 130

If you could take one thing away from your story, what would it be?

DAY 131

List of things that I want to know

DAY 132

Would you rather fight with a lion or a shark? Why?

DAY 133

Have you ever been fired by your teacher?

DAY 134

What's your dream vacation?

DAY 135

What do you like to play videogames with?

DAY 136

What do you dislike about other people?

DAY 137

How would you describe the feeling of something you've never felt before?

DAY 138

Who would you like to know the most? Why?

DAY 139

How do you deal with your own mistakes?

DAY 140

Were you a different person after the experience?

DAY 141

How would you describe the feeling that you are only the symbol or a caricature of what they want you to be?

DAY 142

What is something that you have never tried?

DAY 143

Would you rather be happy about an outcome or miserable about an outcome?

DAY 144

What's your biggest problem now?

DAY 145

What would you prefer to see happen next year?

DAY 146

Tell me about a time when everything went your way.

DAY 147

*If you could spend eternity in the same room with an animal,
what would you think?*

DAY 148

Do you still hope to achieve your goal even after you've learned that this path involves some risks?

DAY 149

What worries do you have?

DAY 150

If you had to choose a favorite dog who is related to you, what would it be?

DAY 151

What is the biggest lie you have ever told anybody?

DAY 152

What is one thing about your life that really stands out?

DAY 153

Why did it go on you so long?

DAY 154

What do you do when someone only has negativity to offer you?

DAY 155

Is there any food you'd like to change eating for the next year? What are those?

DAY 156

What else could you want?

DAY 157

Would you rather have something that smells good but isn't as good as the smell of your favorite candy bar or do you want something sweet and has no aftertaste?

DAY 158

Where's your favorite place to go?

DAY 159

What's something your family does to make you happy?

DAY 160

List of things that I've learned

DAY 161

What's the best approach to resolving conflict?

DAY 162

People you hate to hate:

DAY 163

What happens when you feel like you're going to do something bad?

DAY 164

How would you describe the feeling of being watched by an unknown entity?

DAY 165

What do you do after you go to sleep?

DAY 166

Do you have a fear that you might get bored? Why?

DAY 167

If you could do this in person, what would you do differently?

DAY 168

Say something about your work.

DAY 169

How would you describe the feeling of being gone?

DAY 170

If you could be changed to another personality, who would you be?

DAY 171

How would you describe the feeling of being in the presence of a seemingly unapproachable person?

DAY 172

How would you describe the feeling of being a founder?

DAY 173

Do you prefer your own or others? Why?

DAY 174

What is true love?

DAY 175

What are your thoughts and where do they come from?

DAY 176

Describe the menu for a satisfying dinner in a restaurant.

DAY 177

What is your greatest accomplishment?

DAY 178

If you had to choose one thing to keep from the past, what would it be? Why?

DAY 179

What did you eat for dinner last night?

DAY 180

What is the worst thing you've ever seen in your life?

DAY 181

Should you spend more time with your kids or with your work?

DAY 182

What is the kindest thing that someone has ever done for you?

DAY 183

How would you describe the feeling of being truly connected with the universe around you?

DAY 184

How do you analyze your win rate?

DAY 185

What do you think of the color orange?

DAY 186

What do you spend your time on?

DAY 187

If you could have any three people for lunch, who would they be and why?

DAY 188

What was one memory you've been forced to deal with as a child that you are proud of?

DAY 189

What is the secret to happiness?

DAY 190

What is the one thing you could do about climate change right now?

DAY 191

Describe how you show appreciation to your parents.

DAY 192

How do you deal with that when you say those things?

DAY 193

Who would you trust most to share the truth with you?

DAY 194

What can you do to make yourself feel less alone?

DAY 195

What's the best way to handle people?

DAY 196

Any particular reason you're doing what you're doing now?

DAY 197

What is one thing you will never change?

DAY 198

What's your favorite way to get around?

DAY 199

What's your worst thing to do with your friends?

DAY 200

What has been the most memorable experience of your life?

DAY 201

Who's the person who annoys you the most?

DAY 202

Where would you go for the last time, if the urge ever strikes you?

DAY 203

Would you rather get paid in real-time or monthly? Why?

DAY 204

Has he/she ever taken you with him/her when he/she goes to a sports game or to the theatre? Why?

DAY 205

Would you rather not eat at all? Why?

DAY 206

What's someone else's worst habit?

DAY 207

What's the most difficult part about being you?

DAY 208

What's your favorite past time?

DAY 209

If you were elected President, what do you think would be your most difficult tasks?

DAY 210

What is your first thought when you hear your name mentioned?

DAY 211

Would you rather marry someone extremely attractive or be extremely attractive yourself? Why?

DAY 212

Would you rather fight for the future that you've built or just let the old order crumble? Why?

DAY 213

What do your kids look for in a girlfriend/boyfriend?

DAY 214

What do you admire in yourself and why?

DAY 215

If you suddenly gained the ability to tell whether someone was lying, would you use it?

DAY 216

If all jobs had the same pay and hours, what job would you like to have?

DAY 217

Should junk food be banned from schools? Why?

DAY 218

If you could take the power from everyone, what would you do with it?

DAY 219

What do you want your legacy to be?

DAY 220

How do you help your child make friends?

DAY 221

List of things that we want you to stop doing

DAY 222

Say something that you'd never say to your boss or to the people who are hiring you.

DAY 223

How do you deal with compliments?

____

____

____

____

____

DAY 224

What is one of your life goals?

____

____

____

____

____

DAY 225

What kind of person would you be?

____

____

____

____

____

DAY 226

What is the best and worst place in the world that you've been to?

DAY 227

How do you figure out which is which?

DAY 228

What's the most amazing thing you've experienced?

DAY 229

Do you turn into a robot when you experience failure? Why?

DAY 230

What is the most significant thing you've learned about yourself?

DAY 231

Do you remember the first time you felt "special" as a child? Do you think you feel that way now?

DAY 232

Do you have anything going on that you cannot say? Tell me about it.

DAY 233

How would you describe the feeling of being completely naked with someone you love?

DAY 234

What is the most annoying thing the other person did to you in a conversation?

DAY 235

List of things that I need now

DAY 236

Say something that might make you laugh.

DAY 237

List of things that you want to remember

DAY 238

What do you want your children to know about the future?

DAY 239

What is your most important question from the past?

DAY 240

What's something about your community or country that you are enjoying?

DAY 241

What would you do if you woke up in another country and no one could understand you?

DAY 242

What would it take to put me in your shoes?

DAY 243

What would happen if children ruled the world?

DAY 244

Say something about yourself to anyone who doesn't know who
you are

DAY 245

Why are you doing this?

DAY 246

Are you an emotional being? Why or why not?

DAY 247

If you had to choose one thing from your entire career to give up today, what would it be?

DAY 248

What was the last thing you ate?

DAY 249

What is the one thing that distinguishes you from being average?

DAY 250

What's the most expensive thing you've ever eaten?

DAY 251

Do you feel that the world needs more heroes? Why?

DAY 252

Tell about a time when you had a conflict with a close friend.

DAY 253

What would you be doing without your family?

DAY 254

List of things that will be very useful as a form of therapy

DAY 255

Say something about your situation.

DAY 256

What do you think is the color of your aura?

DAY 257

What do you need to help your children learn about the world?

DAY 258

How has the internet changed your life?

DAY 259

Was there a time when you felt that maybe you should have done something different than you did?

DAY 260

How would you like your pizza?

DAY 261

List of things that are going to kill people

DAY 262

What do your children want when they're feeling afraid?

DAY 263

How strong are your feelings?

DAY 264

What's something you've always thought was true but never said to anyone for fear of being ridiculed?

DAY 265

What are your favorite books that you never read?

DAY 266

Describe your future self

DAY 267

Does the person with the highest desire for life fulfillment align with your life goal and how you want to live?

DAY 268

What is the one thing that will keep you resilient?

DAY 269

What is the best birthday present you could receive?

DAY 270

If you could be someone famous for one hour and it would change your life, who would you be?

DAY 271

When was the last time you thought about how you could improve your job performance?

DAY 272

List of things that you loved this year

DAY 273

Describe a time when you had a conflict with a family member.

DAY 274

What's one song that you think has some of the best lyrics ever written? Write about it.

DAY 275

Do you have any special goals in life? What are those?

DAY 276

Do you still keep an active eye on what goes on in the real world? Why? Why not?

DAY 277

Which friend has had the greatest impact on your life and why?

DAY 278

List of plastic surgeon's favorite foods

DAY 279

What is one thing that you would like to see in your country?

DAY 280

If you had to choose one day to lose the most, which day would
it be?

DAY 281

What do your children want when they're feeling happy?

DAY 282

List of things that may work or not work

DAY 283

What makes you confident that you won't be disappointed?

DAY 284

What is one thing that has been proven to make a huge difference in your life?

DAY 285

Say something about how you're feeling.

DAY 286

What does your best friend do every single day?

DAY 287

Would you rather travel back in time?

DAY 288

What else is your peace?

DAY 289

Why have you become complacent about what you are doing or feeling?

DAY 290

If you could take a step and think about what others will think of you, would you and why?

DAY 291

What is the greatest achievement of your life?

DAY 292

What was the first thing that came to your mind when you thought of that person's last name?

DAY 293

How would you describe the feeling of being not real?

DAY 294

What is the one thing people say they can't do with their time?

DAY 295

Tell me about someone you miss.

DAY 296

Tell about a time when you were tested.

DAY 297

Who do you most despise?

DAY 298

What would you love to have?

DAY 299

What is your greatest ambition?

DAY 300

Do you actively change your habits and behaviors to help the environment? What kinds of things you do?

DAY 301

If you had to choose one color, what would you choose and why?

DAY 302

List of things that were discovered

DAY 303

What's your favorite part of your city?

DAY 304

What's your favorite song that starts with the letter A?

DAY 305

What lessons did you learn from other people's experiences?

DAY 306

How do you deal with criticism if it's something that you know well?

What's the worst thing you've overheard your friends say in front of you?

Which is more important to you, to get things done or to get ahead? Why?

List of things that are available

DAY 310

If you could only go back in time, would you change anything?

DAY 311

What are the risks with your beliefs?

DAY 312

What is your biggest fear that you want to overcome?

DAY 313

How would you say your life has changed?

DAY 314

What is your opinion of people polluting the environment?

DAY 315

How can you help your child deal with rejection?

DAY 316

What is the one thing you really want?

DAY 317

If you had to choose one thing as the defining trait for a woman, what would it be?

DAY 318

Have you ever become hooked on any kind of music?

DAY 319

What is the best compliment you have ever received?

DAY 320

How do you deal with the constant pressure of being an idol?

DAY 321

*If you could choose the three words that will define the next
decade, what would they be?*

DAY 322

Have you ever been in love? Which one? Why?

DAY 323

What is the one thing that has made you interested in writing a book?

DAY 324

Who's the most important person to influence your world?

DAY 325

How would you describe the feeling of being almost completely paralyzed?

DAY 326

The boys were playing video games when… [continue the sentence]

DAY 327

If you could be any rock star of the past or future, who would you be and why?

DAY 328

What is something important to you that you will give up right away if you don't get it right now?

DAY 329

Describe an experience when you should have said no but did not.

DAY 330

What is the best quote you've ever heard?

DAY 331

Do you feel you have the right to be special, just like everyone else? Why?

DAY 332

How many movies do you watch in a year?

DAY 333

If you could look at your life at one instant and give a single sentence to tell to your children and grandchildren, what would you tell them?

DAY 334

What's your favorite thing that you've done so far this year?

DAY 335

Why are you telling the truth?

DAY 336

Is there a time when you will be free of regret? Why?

DAY 337

What do you believe makes you happy?

DAY 338

What is your favorite food in the world?

DAY 339

What are you interested in that most people haven't heard of?

DAY 340

Do you think that your significant other is completely honest
with you? Why or why not?

DAY 341

What can you do to become a leader of the free world?

DAY 342

At 24, what were you doing in your life? Or, if you're not 24 yet, what
are you planning to do or planning to be when you finally reach that
age?

DAY 343

What were your dreams? Are they still dream of a kind?

DAY 344

What can you think of that I can't think of?

DAY 345

If you had to choose one thing to put on your bucket list in the next month, what would it be?

DAY 346

How do you think eating junk food affects you?

DAY 347

What would you do if someone said you did something wrong but you didn't?

DAY 348

Who among your relatives is your favorite?

DAY 349

List of things that are not taking place

DAY 350

Say something you can't say.

DAY 351

Do you believe in evolution? Why or why not?

DAY 352

Does a person's name influence the person they become?

DAY 353

If you had to choose one thing which will give you the biggest advantage in your career, what would it be?

DAY 354

Is everything okay here?

DAY 355

What is the one thing you're not sure of?

DAY 356

What does it feel like to love yourself?

DAY 357

What were the odds that something like this would come up?

DAY 358

Describe a master plan that would make your community a better place to live.

DAY 359

Are you eating enough calories? Why?

DAY 360

What would you prefer if you change your name? Why? Why not?

DAY 361

What's the weirdest thing you've ever done?

DAY 362

Would you rather have all your eggs in one basket or one egg in different baskets?

DAY 363

What is the one thing you do when you lose a game?

DAY 364

Where do you feel most comfortable today?

DAY 365

What would you prefer is the subject of the conversation?

DAY 366

What is a long term goal and how can you achieve it?